RETRO

grade

RETROgrade

poems

Mike Alexander

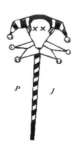

Printed in the United States of America.
Text set in Palatino Linotype.
Cover design by K. A. Thomas
Cover photo by Mike Alexander

P&J Poetics LLC, 1302 Waugh Drive, #197, Houston, TX 77019-3908

ISBN 978-0-9887677-0-6
Library of Congress Control Number: 2013908888

for Marian Lucille Dillinger
& Kitts Bertha Jones

Contents

...with no leſſe nobilitie of loue
Then that which deareſt father beares his ſonne,
Doe I impart toward you for your intent
In going back to ſchoole in Wittenberg,
It is moſt retrogard to our deſire...

CORNUCOPIA

i

My mother urges me to learn the horn.
   "You'll always have a job, no matter where

you find yourself, whatever city, there's
   always a Local." My mother just wants

to raise good union musicians. Her sons
   will pay their dues, & be card-carrying

trumpet-playing men. I don't know how to
   tell her I've dropped my instrument, my mouth-

piece is stuck, & the odor of the valve
   ointment works my gut. She says I'm holding

the horn wrong, it should rise slightly more than
   perpendicular to the ground, & that's

why I have trouble handling some notes,
   why I'm slow at fingering my sixteenths.

My mother says, "just try it from the top,
   take it to the coda, then start again."

ii

At first the valves stand open, then I close
  the first & the third together, the first

& the second, the first alone, & then
  the way is clear again, again I close

the first & the second, then the second
  alone, & then again the way is clear,

I'm scaling up a major scale, but as
  I force my air into these close quarters,

trap-doors, dead-ends, I strain to pitch myself
  one half-step higher than I could before,

I plunge myself into a labyrinth
  where passages slide open & slam shut

without ever delivering the note
  to end all notes, I reach with my last breath

into the dark bell, cornucopia
  from which others pull such unearthly fruit.

iii

I'm buying CDs, all kinds, jazz, swing, ska,
    dixieland, rhythm & blues, soul, & lounge.

I rotate the top four or five, & then
    replace them with another four or five.

Impulse, Milestone, Reprise — make me turn east
    & face Decca, a subterranean

intensity rears up from the subways,
    a crescendo, & I see the faces

in a flourish, it's Louie, Freddie, Miles
    & Chet, each one halo'd by a blue spot,

in isolation or in concert, horns
    muted or blatant, the brass taste is back

in my mouth, in my CD player
    where numbers spin in perpetuity,

I imagine I'm the darkness, playing
    audience to those who turn in the light.

iv

Confectionery sugar caps your glass
    of arctic vodka. I sip the currant-

red elixir at my lip. The trumpet
    soloist, not two feet away, has clamped

a horn to his kisser, his embouchure,
    as if to drink a horn's-worth of alpine

ice-water, having scaled a severe cliff-
    face. His face puffs, an old cartographer's

caricature of the wind god's bluster —
    his eyes clench shut, blind to the room & its

distractions. He's putting all of his guff,
    his blood & his bone, into the one riff,

& if he falls, that piercingly high C
    he's clinging to won't save him. I'm waiting

for his lip to crack. This idiot, this
    jack-in-the-box. O God. I envy him.

v

Buried amid toys & appliances
    with warrantees long since expired,

guns & jewelry of uncertain faith,
    bugle, cornet, trumpet, flugelhorn

stand at attention, up-ended, condemned
    souls in a junk-shop ensemble. Tarnish,

not gold, their finishes, as their coffins
    gather dust under the counter. Empty.

Clarion, French horn, Baritone. I start
    to quake as I pass by this abandoned

trumpery. Whatever breath of life once
    warmed these metallic chalices long since

split out the spit valve. Still, each one harbors
    a hope of resurrection, & resounds

with hallelujahs in its quiet heart.
    To rise & be played at the final Trump.

CITY LIFE

If asked to relocate,
you could set up shop
in the city of Ur,

teach yourself
to read & write
cuneiform,

apply to work
for bureaucrats
housed in the sky,

match jars
of jasmine oil
to bills of lading,

ignore the roar
of restless camels
at night,

drink grain
with gods
on holy days,

follow weekly
installments
of Gilgamesh,

blame nomadic
tribes for cutbacks
at the temple,

covet new
metals, Cretan
axe-heads, saffron,

sleepwalk the long
shadows of
sandstone giants,

an abacus your palm
pilot, a clay tablet
your laptop,

the sky
turning above you
your cable,

a hundred thousand
stars, & nothing
to watch.

THE CRUISE SHIP

You have become a ship for parasites — Kunitz

As fleas once rode the backs of rats
across a filthy Mediterranean,
carrying bubonic doubt
into ports ripe
for religious upheaval,
guilty in armpit, guilty in crotch,
you have traveled.
Climbing
the first wave,
falling
on the next,
like a brochure
with the best intentions,
till you yourself are in the picture.
You hurry
to the oldest
parts of the port city.
You sample the locals.
Your ship anchors
a few hours,
but for those few hours,
it darkens the water, the air,
like you, an invader, a bloodstained idol.
You buy a snapshot of the cathedral.
You order a hamburger
with extra pickles
at the closest
café to the harbor.

Your eyes swim in the mirror
behind a phalanx of open bottles,
already saying your goodbyes.
You swap spit with a statue,
then
back to the boat.
If there were time you might have
attended mass, you might have seen
the café preside over low tide.
You might
have come to hate
hordes
like yourself, infecting
the already
deficient immune system
of history. Thank god there isn't time.

THE GREAT YEAR

We wake up the same
as any other day,
blind, naked, hurrying
to put the bathroom door
between us. We know
the day, set
in motion, spins us
out of our shared orbit.

Plato might try to console
the parted lovers with a story
about caves & philosophic
light, but then Freud
would be quick to explain
the darker overtones,
hysteria, birth trauma,
fantasies of sexual
adequacy.

       No wonder
the working world steers
clear of either pole
as fast as it can spin.
We wake, & it's
too late for aubades,
refusals, leaving that door
open.

Plato says
all cycles come full circle,
somewhere in his dialogues,
I don't care where.
Only that we still hope
for moving bodies parted
in individual circles
to approach, to recognize
each other, returning
to warm sheets.

IN STASIS

Ten meters from the ride's end
    the power gone
        out,

like fundamentalists
anticipating the End of Days,
    thrill seekers forced
        to wait,

locked in, feet dancing over
the dead drop that
disappears in the dance;
        the metaphor no longer
        likens them to astronauts,

but to the hanged,
the fairgrounds darker than deep space,
tested, finally,

with time enough to doubt the spelling
of apocalypse, the rapture of
mechanics.

TEMPLO EL REFUGIO

No, the saints are not marching.
Marching in heat like this would be
a sin. In heat like this, every noonday is
a sabbath. No one would dare to dishonor,
disinherit, dissemble, steal or dismember
in heat like this. No one covets or plays
false at this temperature. There are
no other gods. Aluminum chairs
unfold, the only graven images
left sitting out in expectation, a perfect
attendance, too absolute to be seen.
No one parks around the lot perimeter.
No one trespasses. Its signboard singes like
firewood over its furnace of a portico,
over the service at which saints
alone take their seats. How graceful
they would have to be to march between
those fiery chairs without knocking into one.

CRAZY JANE & THE CRACK PIPE

God sings thru a hollow pipe.
He sings, & on spiked heels, I lurch
along the crosswalk's double stripe.
   On this rock I build my church.

I have no miracles to confess.
No altar linen to besmirch.
No sacristy where I undress.
   On this rock I build my church.

A lipstick saint, a limestone whore,
yet searches, hopeless, as I search
for keys to open heaven's door.
   On this rock I build my church.

GO WESTWARD, HOMERIC ANGEL

Odysseus, turn right. Two eighty five
north stretches straight until it hits the sky.
You wonder if you'll make it back alive,
or wander till your Trojan horses die.

You trusted in odometer & map,
& never asked which deities to thank.
You've led yourself alone into this trap,
one eye ahead, one eye fixed on the tank.

No man, Odysseus, drew this dry divide
across the ashes of an ancient sea,
the Texas flatland interstate you ride,
Cyclops blindsided by geography.

The sky's on fire. The highway never ends.
The gods are laughing hard, as night descends.

SIRENS ANSWER

You filled your ears with sealing wax, & sailed
within an inch of transcendental song,
a glory coveted as one among
the numbered wonders of the sea: fish-tailed,

we bared our human breasts, as we regaled
your vessel with our singing, singing long
through your prosaic skulls. You did us wrong
to claim in your accounts our shanties failed.

Although you dulled our melodies to keep
what arguments you treasured most intact,
our musicking is subtler & deep

enough to wash away the dregs of fact —
we sing your darkest voyage as you sleep,
until you wake, eyes leaking, voices cracked.

WAX

It took me nearly a week to find
my way back out of the blind alley.
The marquee over a waning museum
marked the old Quarter, stiffened
figures displayed in paraffin
tableaux, not the ragtime
heart of a living Orleans.
Of the dead, one Creole
on a sparse battlefield had a pump
working its chest cavity,
belying the dull features of his waxen
compatriots. No sigh, no curse
from the duke or from Napoleon,
splashing about in his bath, or from
quadroon whores condemned to solicit
at all hours in scarlet recreation.
Even tortured slaves kept the silence.
Just as well the Dungeon was still
under reconstruction, closed
to walk-in traffic. If I had seen
those famous monsters of filmland
alongside the worst the years could do,
imprisoned in sealant, tamed & tempered
by universal fear of the Great Fire,
it would not have been possible
to escape, to return, to tell the tale.

RE:ENACTMENT

i. AUGURY

When I stood
   stalled in the bus
      kiosk at the curb

I thought
   all vehicles could
      recognize a good

Jerseyman in
   passing, & that
      some among them

would stop, like
   the bus in its hour,
      & take me

as far as our
   trade routes
      coincided, drop me

elsewhere, as if
   all roads were
      interchangeable,

& not as single
    as the implicating
      whorls

of fingertips.
    I stood & flirted
      with the rush

of cars until
    my bus arrived;
      I boarded, paid

& fantasized until
    my stop. But
      now I drive,

the steering wheel
    at my dashboard
      drives home

the difference. Transient
    faces at the curb
      mean

less than roadkill,
    less than the light,
      the one

incendiary light
　　hanging, mid-air,
　　　unchanged.

ii. THE CLOSTER HORSEMAN

Warships scuttle like roaches
    under the fog; a shadowy

vanguard infests the narrow
    clefted Palisades —

A foregrounded puddlesplash
    punctuates a horse-

hoof on the gallop. Occult knowledge
    whitening the eyes of

mount as well as rider —
    as Anonymity comes to

the rescue, as Name encroaches —
    Which to worship?

iii. PROLEGOMENON

G Washington Br (I-95),
early on

the rise as always,
surveys the damage done to

his map over breakfast. Across
the North River,

Fort Washington Ave
in ruins. Now, the city's

outward ramparts wear banners
of the largest known

expeditionary
force, & as word has it,

Great British pine barrens
scale the high Palisades;

we forfeit
fortifications, the bulk of

our supply to feed
the Old World. "I am wearied,"

he has written the night before,
"almost to death

with the retrograde
motion of things." Washington,

to iconographers,
towers in his stirrups,

hurdles the distance
in three quarters of an hour —

Back down on street level, Greene's men
know well enough

how to run at their own discretion.
New orders

echoe above the Pandemonium.
Forget

about provisions.
"Some hundred barrels of flour,

most of our cannon
& a considerable

parcel of tents
& baggage." Forget utensils,

ledgers, correspondence,
penmanship & place name,

this property calls out
to us. Listen &

follow
these directions to the final letter.

iv. MONUMENT PARK

As windshield wipers scrape the glass, our hourglass
distorted lot, cars corralled, we locals rally
down at this strip of Fort Lee, by Bridgeview deli,
to buy foodstuffs, combustibles, marked-down items,

& precipitate weather, between Palisades
& Parker, stock up on the essential tabloids,
street maps, greeting cards & occasional verses,
scratch-offs & videotape cornucopias,

ransack the disheveled shelves, scramble for cover,
as if under fire, as if the driving rain
scratched across corraded petroleum filmstock,
as yellowed, as melodramatic as *The Birth*

of a Nation, in all its insatiate frenzy,
this action, this onslaught, somehow correlative
to these customers hard at their customary
sprees, a cast of thousands, cut to extreme close-up,

all their faces wet, their eyes wild, their mouths working,
& look at the captions — under new management,
thirty minute limit, next day service, take out
& delivery, twenty four hour banking,

grand opening, residential parking only,
violators will be summonsed, immobilized
& towed, this last ordinance (ninety-thirty-one)
preserves the quietude of English street, due east

from the lot, higher ground, its houses bivouacked
against the rain, against encroachment, red brickface
& graying aluminum, suburban estates
united in various states of disrepair,

sequestered by shade trees & trellises, landscaped
indifferently, shy, revolutionary
artifacts sleeping just below top soil,
& Glory still clinging to a flag pole above

one garden, on the grounds of a fortress first known
as *Constitution*, then as *Lee*, & then unknown —
the gentry here defend their nonpartisanship,
eschew full regalia, affect no causes,

neither Whig, nor Tory, swearing by regular
hours, frequenting malls, scarcely voting, & yet
their nursemaids brave inclemency, even in
determined rain, carry the nurslings in their care

down to this monument, in order that the young
may play below the words cut on the bluestone base
of this Rebelmen statue — two patriots, two scouts,
keep watch as if this rock were still under attack,

alert as sprint-runners or silent celluloid
cliffhangers, while cars & bulldozers claim the last
open spaces, stop & change places at quarter-
hour intervals, filling meters one quarter

at a time, for that's how we measure historic
rainfall, while monumental Palisades erupt
in thunder — a battery of mortar cannon
redoubles over Fort Lee like a starting gun.

v. MAIN STREET

Of the Parking
    Authority, Fort Lee,
        I sing,

an epic space
    in front of the News Bar.
        Pick up

a brevé or
    an iced espresso,
        Journalist!

Update the latest
    disturbance
        in the river

valley provinces.
    There's a privy
        in the rear,

whereat I thought,
    let's recommence
        this Iliad —

How did that
    anchorman engage
        his reportage?

An uneasy
    détente, a sulking
        in the ranks,

as I remember,
    or was that the
        fourth chapter

of Ulysses?
    What does it tell,
        the graffiti

on this relatively
    fresh paint-job?
        Was the War

fought over
    where a standing
        army could secure

its vehicles?
    Park your car in
        an unloading

zone, & it's
    Battalion! to the
        Right about — Face!

There's this book,
    Baron von Steuben's
        "regulations

for the order &
    discipline of the
        troops," which

tells
    a different tale.
        No accounting for gods

or heroes.
    By other reports
        the fort withstood

ten years of siege,
    but this book depicts
        disorderly

conduct, describes
    a full half-circle,
        a retread.

Achilles skipped
    on his commanding
        officer.

The Son of Man tried
        to back out
                of the garden.

The Hero
        of Brooklyn Heights
                officiated

a full strategic
        withdrawal. It's
                the same here.

You bypass
        the Post Office &
                the Library.

You follow Main
        until it abandons
                Fort Lee,

descends into
        the Hollows & runs
                further down

into less
        congested lowlands.
                What news travels

after that?
    You've got your
        coffee, your paperback

drill manual, a
    Hagstroms &
        copious notes.

Our first step taken
    toward sovereignty
        was a step

backwards.
    We ran, as we run
        now, backsliding

to our cars.
    Put it in reverse
        & turn around.

The going's slow.
    Store fronts fall in
        on either side,

close rank & pledge you
    no allegiance.
        After all,

you're leaving,
    you will soon forget,
        you will unlearn

the revolutionary
    songs that once
        you sang.

What do you need
    to know about
        the Crisis, now

miles behind
    you, the windshields
        blinded by tickets,

the sack of your
    city's Parking
        Authority,

Main, & those
    who remain in one
        another's arms?

vi. GRAND AVENUE

You'd turn upstream if you were still on a river,
cut a sharp right to shake the rain out of your eyes,
lose whatever headlights dog your wake, whatever

limousined escort jackals you to Paradise,
indecently departed citizen. You'd turn
the wheel hard to the right, glance but once or twice

in your rearview, to catch the high-beams that still burn
your retinas. Another hellish light. Ignore
the battle-cars you lack the battle-scars to earn.

The more you fight the wheel in your grip, the more
the old complaints adhere to you, the more your ghosts
persist in plaguing you, & everywhere, the war

you fight for independence befouls & exhausts
your personal reserves. Station your car ahead
of a lengthy procession of griefs. Pitch signposts

to protect the Neighborhood, up & back, unread,
with pictograms where foot soldiers, conscripted, cross
a pedestrian walkway of the walking dead —

Bandage up your bleeding feet. Refuse to discuss
the deadening pain, every step of which refers
to a page in your pocket book of Exodus.

Study the lines on the asphalt, chapter & verse,
for the ones who know your book, cover to cover,
wait now for word to come from the back of a hearse.

vii. PALISADES AVENUE

Lunch-hour shift turns green, full to capacity.
Imagine that the shop windows implode, & spill
a shower of commodities. But I review

my previous employment history, dressed as
bookseller, bank teller, cashier, accounting clerk,
& temp, & find there's no great Vegas-style payoff

in the next scene — no express elevators up
in this city. Take off the emerald glasses.
The only job openings are part-time starter

positions. The hours, crap. Hey, don't get me wrong.
There's nothing I wouldn't do for king & country.
When Washington's troops stop by for a few supplies,

I'll be the first behind the register, to say,
"will that be cash or charge, sir? No American
Express, I'm sorry, only Visa/Mastercard."

Deliver us this day's complaints to management.
Check the receipts. Whose pen & ink complexion's on
the dollar's face? Let the president break a sweat.

viii. LIBERTY ROAD

A snapshot, freely captured by disposable
camera along the side of Liberty Road,
by insufficient light: alabaster statue
of Liberty, barely clothed, polytheistic
figure, life-size, dancing her celebratory
dance-steps, whirling a veil,
    a parti-colored veil,

about her body, swirling the diaphanous
crescent arc of her veil, an end-parenthesis
to a parenthetical aside, ascribing
dithyrambic meter to patriotic dances,
her veil, a scythe, a Saracen sword, a sheath,
a silhouette, dancing
    the dance of seven veils,

unveiling, as Liberty's often depicted
bare-breasted on a battlefront, an Amazon,
a majorette twirling a baton on parade,
her veil, a flag, & the Goddess herself, a girl
exploding on the street on the 4th of July,
a fireworks display
    on the 4th of July,

a color guard, a cavalcade of fife & drum,
a drill team executing its double-time march
down the dividing line of a rain-riddled street,
a locale whose architectural legends range
from early- to mid- to late-Americana,
an abstract in concrete,
    Liberty drops her veil,

in mid-Revolution, steps from her pedestal,
a chimera to one side of Liberty Road,
& poses for a camera to dispose of
as it will, her likeness, as icon, as Vestal.
The available daylight barely suffices.
One shutter click, she dances —
    toward the Armory.

ix. NEW BRIDGE

It cannot rain forever,
even this close to Hackensack,
it cannot militate forever,
even this close to the water,
it cannot close us out forever,
even this forbidding briar,

aluminum arrowheads,
these imperatives — STOP —
NO STOPPING OR STANDING —
YIELD — U TURN — ONE WAY —
cannot obscure, cannot obviate,
ancestral places, ancestral retreats.

The dance screeches to a halt.
Cars pile up, cars & their parts,
hubcaps, tires, rare & antique,
stall in this bone-yard, & accelerate
no further. No thru-traffic,
but for Historical Society use.

A commemorative plaque
weathers names & dates of
freeholders & socialites, whose
patronage sanctifies this real
estate, this sandstone homestead,
this sword that cannot be withdrawn.

The past is present under
arthritic birches. An apartment
complex, the Stueben Arms,
holds in its arms a former
barracks. Wet grackles serve
sentry duty for the drillmaster.

Perform a figure eight,
three times in succession,
a dozen times, or two dozen.
It's an instinctual response,
an ingrained patriotism,
a loyalty for the soil.

It's just about dusk
as the head of the troops
rides down to the narrow
tidewater stream, the dock
beyond church & courthouse.
We continue on foot.

The last house on the left
looks to be too small to house
its story. Our expectations cannot
fit through the doorway, brush
against a bare ceiling. Old books,
tableware, quiltwork, pastimes.

Ancient by American
standards, the landing at
New Bridge casts its iron
shadow-work over white silt
riverbed; closed to visitors,
the General, in particular.

Two PSE&G trucks &
a chain link, edged with barbed
wire: DANGER HIGH VOLTAGE
EQUIPMENT. Slick tarmac &
transformers bring the sky
to ground. We shuck our shoes.

Then, at last, the white birds,
the slow water, a refuge where
"the mill, once powered by the tides,
burned in 1852 after a century of service."
The house in its serviceable vantage
grants us this recess, this garden,

even this forbidding briar.
It cannot close us out forever,
even this close to the water,
it cannot militate forever,
even this close to Hackensack,
it cannot rain forever.

x. AWAY

Turn about & turn back
    the way you came
    passing
under Seventeen. Turn
left, where the light
turns red.

    Turn left,
& follow through
the next two lights,
back the
way you came,
    & at the third light, before
    the rail-

road
crossings, take a right,
facing back the way you
came, face
Eighty. Take a right, a left,
    & get back

onto Eighty, accelerate,
    set your headlights
by the highway, & take it back
the way you came.

THE GOD

Starved for something
I hadn't gotten yet
from the books, the cards,
the gatherings,

I salivated
in the courtyard
behind Enchantments
(East 9th) to think

it was my turn to represent
the god. I knelt through
the hour-long ritual,
standing only

to draw the circle,
where to the east a tile
of porcelain peaked over
brickface

walls, where west
a satyr fountain
ran dry, where north
all uptown uprose,

where south the store
burned its dragon's
blood incense. I blessed
the salt & the bread,

then bit into the offering
like Pan, impatient for
the end of business
& for revels to begin.

If I did anything wrong,
it was to wear those horns
back home to Jersey,
where no one could see.

CHARYBDIS

I bring a load of whites — wool sacrifice,
our lost cotton mesh, our warmth, sweat-stained,
reptilian skins shucked off, that we replace

in secret, streaked with venom, rattle-brained
secretions from the grass, a tire's screech,
convulsions. Working in the basement, chained,

a tool bench, badly-stocked, just out of reach,
beside the storage bin below the stairs —
I lean into the Whirlpool, adding bleach

& Tide to gym socks folded into pairs,
an extra change of sheets, large undershirt
& underwear. In antiseptic chores,

our nightmares gather strength. Like week-old dirt,
our whites show the regrets, the faded vows,
perpetual mortgage of a ground-in hurt.

I've tried to pass for the exemplary spouse,
while turning like a termite in the wood,
like cracks in the foundation of the house,

I feel the mortar wash away for good.
I feel exposed to adder-lidded eyes.
I feel the Whirlpool rocking in my blood.

ACROSS & DOWN

She takes a Sunday ritual, like
crosswords over instant coffee,
& makes it last the week.

She calls clues from the kitchen
to anyone in earshot. She consults
a dictionary. She asks over the phone.

What's "dementia?"

Here's how many letters she has.
Out of ten, the first gets "the first grade."

The second starts what lovers called her.
The third, "the sleeping letter,"
& that's
the last she's sure of.
After that, she needs help.

The empty squares inside a larger
square stump her, her
dissolution.

Whatever guess she pencils down
disproves another guess she's made across.

Gaps in the messaging network.

The in-between letters get tangled
in the toxic silk of synaptic chemicals
she couldn't spell when well,
serotonin, acetylcholine, —

Medical books prescribe the drawing
of magic squares, as they have done
since Asclepius, except that now
the numbers aren't numbers,
but genetic code.

By filling in letters,
doctors scry through her unraveling.

Even so, the books never
spell it out. The last letter wants
to be either
plural or possessive,
but she's left with an over-
abundance of Amyloid plaques,
as arcane as those
in consultation offices.

She gets ten letters, & while
she tries to add them together,
she forgets to shut out the lights.

FERMATA

I walk in as my mother plays "A Long,
Long Way from Home" from memory. The keys
kneel gracefully beneath her hands, the song

obeys her touch with such apparent ease,
that I am marveling at her technique,
not the progressive state of her disease.

While playing, she can keep in tempo, speak
coherently, & smile. She must have played
the same piece every day of every week.

Away from her piano-barricade
she'll talk as if the words do not belong
to her, but to the Alzheimer's, to trade

a gesture or a fluting of her tongue
for once familiar melodies gone wrong.

LETHE

She asks each time I call, when I will visit her,
& asks me for the number I am calling from,
she scrawls it down again although it is the same
exactly as it was the time I called before,

she notes it in her date book, same as when she lived
by dates, recitals, classes, calls, documented,
a book for every year, she keeps these books at hand,
to travel through the days, secure, & every year,

she leaves a book somewhere, & retraces her steps,
she burns the world to find it, to the last hotel,
returns to the airline customer service desk,
empties her purse on the counter, & starts again

to pencil in the family history, she keeps
the family tree, uprooted & replanted
in the wide margins of a date book, burial
places, bloodlines, marriages, to each its entry,

& she carries a crossword taken from the Times
of the previous week, folded four-square & tucked
into her book, to mark where she is, & when she
uses the phone, she has to hold the book open,

one-handed, to scratch in the new apocrypha,
hunched over the pages like Michelangelo's
Sibyl, all her prophesies concerning the past,
she asks, when I call again, asks for the number,

& I sigh against the receiver, deliver
the ritual formula, repeat the number,
& remind her, & I don't want to remember
the last time I visit her, she opens her purse,

lays out the photographs like ancient tarot cards,
rows of relatives arranged in yellowed gardens,
glaring with squinted eyes out of blurred afternoons,
oxidized pigments from an indistinct ceiling,

almost as mythic as the major arcana,
her fingers pausing over the creased pantheon,
waiting in open anticipation for her
to start the litany, to name the names, to call

the distant cousins close, when she stops herself,
lips parted already, marbled eyes already
turning to ask who these faces are, these strangers,
& she starts to ask why I, another stranger,

smile at her, & she smiles in return, the pictures
in her hand forgotten, autumn colors, ochre,
burnt orange, sunset, twilight, penny-ante postcards,
place-keepers, & there's no way that I can tell her

who they are, or who I am, a few creased faces
I usher back into her purse before I leave,
her days, days at a glance, the leaves annotated
in her distinctive scrawl, her own hand washed away,

the pages clean again, her open date book blank,
she says she can't remember where she had it last,
disconnected, she wades off into the river,
& I drop the receiver into its cradle.

PAPER DOLLS

Stripping
her clothes
off, she kicks
aside his dirty
laundry,
to uncover
a box of magazines
underneath. The nude
on top is spread to
show herself
    hollow.

This, she frowns,
is what he sees

— puppets he can
cram his fist
into —

a string of paper
dolls, contortionists,
unresisting & supple,
joined together
at the staple.

In double
exposure, she
falls forward into
the bottomless
box. Below
her, she sees
flames in naked
flower,
    spreading.

CAMDEN AQUARIUM

The dharma sea lion sunbathes
above the lower rungs of the food-
chain, as even overdone tongue
eats & therefore creates.

Propped atop his pedestal,
prior to his meridian feeding,
the obsidian bull seal
broods like an emperor

over the variety in his diet,
& contemplates the protuberance
of his navel. Lesser seals nibble
into view, & re-submerge.

Lunch-hour matinee audiences
salivate, behind concrete. They forget
the Aquarium gate, inside of which
great sea turtles fly, electric eels

dance, & sand sharks
double up & flex muscular
fins. They forget to taste
the singing of speckled trout.

AQUARIUS

Be the crystal cup that even as it shatters rings -- Rilke

Borne out
on the appropriate hour
a busload breaks free of its building.

There is no air here,
where initiates hold that memory
of breath, held without assurance of
what should be salvaged in that holding,
held until the holding hurts.

The commuter
of a thousand faces —
call him Parzival — faces
a dark window, in which he sees
blackened brick & sea gulls
haunting uncollected trashbins
    as solid evidence of his descent.

    • • •

The city resurfaces
now, an island across the river.
Parzival's eye
courses along the margin
where buildings, etched

along the shoreline, become
water & then return to rock.
The horizon
waits in the west like
a royal wedding, a predetermined
ending toward which the sky does not move.

    • • •

He rests his shield in
the rack overhead & reclines
his seat at the touch of a button.

A bell is rung.
A young woman dressed
in blood-colored dress, her face
dimly lit, comes up the aisle bearing
a sort of serving dish before her.
Another follows with a javelin
leaking a wake of blood.

The bus lets them off & continues
wordlessly into the evening,

Parzival dares not ask direction
of this traveling silence,
so much like church.

But what is the object
of such worship?

What congregation rides
public transportation through
the heartland without a prayer?

    • • •

Each passenger stops
the bus in turn to exhibit
a particular wound, touches
a hand or foot, indicates
a sore in the side or
a genital disorder.

Each carries a complaint inside
that never closes.

It goes on like this.

Each according to schedule
descends to earth & plants
a last step into the headlights,
crowned with something like grief,
something like a miraculous
scavenge.

    • • •

Headlights & streetlights
& ghostlights configure into one
wandering constellation.

The Grail charges the air,
the drinkers of air &
the mixture of ingredients
therein.

It imparts knowledge
to those it causes sleep.

There is a redness in it
like the veins of a burning rose.

Last on the bus,
Parzival undoes his damaged

armor & hides his eyes
against the lost remains of daylight

  seeing again
the lance & the dish.

• • •

Arise, Parzival.
This is your stop
within walking distance
of fruition. Arise & breathe.

Though at first it looks
an unlikely site for ritual, see
how the signs are turned.

See how the random birds
have chosen this spot
to look for seed.

Arise & tell the driver
this is where you rest,
& be sure to ask

what questions
complete the quest.

VEGETAL CHRIST

We left off watering
      the bare poinsettia
the last of its red hearts
dropping bruised to the rug

We should've hid it
      as we were told
confine it to solitary
through summer

deprive it its
      absolution
sol invictus
we counted its sins
blind in the broom closet

freed from its crypt
with advent of autumn
it opened its wounds again
      incarnate solstice
beside the television.

SHAHRAZAD

Your head set on an ancestral server
lets the fables bleed from your lips to stain
silk coverlets — I'd swear to surrender

my kingship if I could to feed again
on your fabulous tales, your fantasies
as ornate as your strategies were plain.

I wanted to live as in your stories,
not droplet by droplet, not dawn by dawn.
I drank the wine whole with its mysteries.

I drank the dark, & as the darkness then
swelled into blood, I drank in its blood-thick
silence. I've tasted one thousand nights & one

since you sang me the tale of the lunatic
emperor & his beheaded courtesan.

MS. PACMAN

You were the queen of the arcade, fast talk,
quick temper, darling of my college days –
When your entanglements betrayed a maze
of dead-end arguments, you'd take a walk

(*a-wawk-a-wawk-a-wawk-a-wawk-a-wawk…*)
then double-back with a voracious phrase
to turn the tables on that hungry gaze,
an adolescent male's unpleasant sulk.

You were the campus deity of choice,
an Aphrodite to the lucky few,
a Circe, a Diana, to rejoice
in the luckless pining of your retinue.

What appetite, what love allowed your voice
the art to turn the men around you blue?

FIRST CONFESSION

A miserable childhood? Yes, of course,
that says it all, one retrospective look.
Accused, I use unnecessary force.

I pummel myself without remorse,
my sucker punch, my merciless right hook.
A miserable childhood. Yes, of course.

Then, marriage & expedient divorce,
a fool-proof recipe I overcook.
Accused, I use unnecessary force.

Is this a staged confession to endorse
a Gospel, a Koran, a Pentateuch,
a miserable childhood? Yes. Of course,

I saddle up my daily hobbyhorse.
White queen's bishop takes red king's rook.
Accused, I use unnecessary force.

I post my package bomb to megastores,
my preemptive strike, an inoffensive book.
A miserable childhood, yes, of course.
Accused, I use unnecessary force.

DECODER RING

Super Sugar Crisps consecrate my kitchen floor,
as I pull from newly opened box my prize,
a secret decoder ring. The pieces snap together,
an alphabet on a ring that fits around my thumb,
but looks like it could tell the orbit of planets,
or unravel fingerprints under a microscope.
With my secret decoder ring, I decipher
the Volkswagen's license plate, chalk
on the asphalt, the serial code on my bike.
I translate any word into its inner arithmetic.
I fill spiral notebooks with qabalistic equations.
My name (thirteen, nine, eleven, five) which
adds up to thirty-eight, can turn one notch
to the right, into fourteen, ten, twelve, & six,
& I disappear into my codified gematria.
Whatever I decode, I can code again.
I spin the dial, my schoolwork falls behind,
my cereal bowl encompasses the Milky Way,
life breaks into the seven basic food groups.
My vision blurs, & when it clears, I see the earth
itself, a decoder ring, spinning to riddle out
a number like infinity. I see my parents
as number-clusters, multiplying & dividing,
some assembly required, batteries not included.

I see check out lines at the Stop n' Shop.
The future is written on the cover of TV guide.
The revolution will be colorized by TNN.
I tremble at all my decoder ring reveals to me.
The cultural cleansing of my people begins, before
I ever get the chance to answer the $64,000 question,
before Steve Allen ridicules Kerouac to his face,
before Noxzema, before Spic n' Span, before
                                        Pillsbury,
before Ed Sullivan goes off the air, before bed-time.
Women no longer wear spotless cotton gloves.
Men stop wearing hats that smell of Arthur Miller.
My mother takes my comic books away for good,
my DC Giant Batman annual tossed in the trash,
Green Lantern, my light & my protection, burnt out,
complexions of future generations sacrificed
to Aveda ritual, age cream, botox, scarification,
as angels execute double-helix kama-sutra
configurations to tempt the Super Sugar Bear,
out of diddling with his own secret ring.
I wake up, having missed the best cartoons,
the cornerstone of any nutritious eschatology.
My head is stamped with the Bear's trademark.
Copyright in Excelsis. Free gift inside.
Act now while supply lasts.

CANTICLE OF THE SEVENTH MONTH

There was a great obsession with water
in those days.

      Mosquitoes monitored
the local pool. Hyperglycemic kids
cannonballed in, two at a time.
A chunk-white cherub swooned into
chlorinated blue, after a two-toned

Venus in pigtails rose from the deep end.
What vigilance. Disposable youths in cut-offs
& clogs parade through arcades to murder
one another, & quench bloodthirst
with Dr. Pepper.

      No one cared about anything
less than the repair of the air conditioning.
We burned Freon in the pitch of those afternoons,
& what peculiar girl stepped out in her
nightgown to check thermostats?

It is said: a man died on the east beach,
carried off by a sunspot of naked valkyries,
& children buried him under sand castles.
He wasn't found until the third day.

A day of rain

    & who doesn't
dream of resurrection in July?

THE FOG MACHINE

A watermark of bug repellent
stains bark raw, suburban charm
against a fear that climbs our maples
every seventh year.
The storm it wards is not
    the sort that rains.

When caterpillars come,
no one explains, & so
we chew up what we overhear
of evening news, & play the rest by ear.
A haze infests
    the backyard of our brains.

One day, above
the sun's unnerving grind,
we hear a truck. We hop our bikes
& ride like angels
    in the cloud it leaves behind,

a fog through which we fly
in reckless pride,
daredevils, bombardiers,
no hands & blind, inhaling
    the perfume of pesticide.

DU TEMPS PERDU

i

A good son
keeps his developed
smile, Kodak, regardless,
staring into the flash cube sun
behind her. I flinch,

my jaw unclenching, out of focus.
She places herself so she blazes.
It hurts to look at her,
even after she takes away
my glasses, my tortoise shell,

& backs me up to the studio wall.
No blindfold. No final words.

ii

Over the mantel,
dark presences, human trophies

of a great white hunter, glossy-eyed,
decorate our living

room, the television-flicker
over our faces. Great-grandmother

sits for her portrait, corseted, Victorian.
Our mother, a girl, unblinking in military

uniform, holds at rigorous attention,
clarinet in gloved grasp. All our

baby pictures, graduations, framed,
crowd too close to radiance.

iii

Victorians commissioned
child portraits,

captured in velveteen diminutive
of adult couture, plush, hand-
tailored to the tiniest detail, a favorite

toy, a complimentary nosegay, a grammar
book, caught in mid-play or mid-study,

impeccably mannered, color-
coordinated, rouge blush discretely

added to pallid cheeks with the painter's

brush, anything to help surviving
family remember.

iv

Early photographers hid under
a cloak of darkness, pried a lens cap
off its lens, then asked the bright world

to stop in its tracks, at least until
the cap was back in place. How many
lives did your exposures save from death?

Primitive souls, stolen, sold on a black
market, my tribe,
we squint, blur, sabotage

your attempts to take us alive. We know
what hungers hide behind the cloak.

WHAT'S AT STAKE

First, there's the boring wait on night to fall,
or light to fail -- & light is more resilient
than one would think. Each dawn is like withdrawal.

Whoever said the dead move fast was brilliant;
that being said, it isn't very often
they try to bring their habits up to speed
with what's been going on outside the coffin.

Few night schools teach what Nosferatu need.
Blood is the life, but still it tastes like death,
a greed that's savored best in isolation,
a grief that clings like garlic to the breath.
Each kill is tantamount to escalation.

The jugulars we drain, night after night,
can never cleanse that first inhuman bite.

TALK

Corduroy, rather
than velveteen,
but still a carrier.

Tactile enough for
the infantile grip
it fascinates. It

fastens itself to
the child. The cast
of its cranium holds

one expressionless
expression. Its
vocabulary, all

pre-recorded,
runs on cat-
gut raveling

through the
eye-hole in its
back. It confesses

like the subject of
a sentence, the
same crimes with

every priming of the
lash. It protests
its affections,

affectations only
a child could suffer
itself to believe.

It was my first,
my oldest brother.
I knew it detested

the drawl of ripcord.
I knew it hated
the sound of its voice.

THEATRE

In my days of childhood programming,
days of compulsory song —
we took the cardboard puppet theater,
cut with holes for curtain rods —
a cost-effective Punch & Judy show.

We stood it upright,
stood inside, & made believe
we stood inside a private television,
& let the backyard stand for the nation.

Rhododendrons hushed
the audience,
as we struck one hand against
the other,
& the rioting began.

A gold-stitched king was deposed,
& princess Barbie, his youngest daughter,
denuded. An armless GI Joe
led legions of Snoopies
to storm the invisible fortress.

We broke open bags of toy plastic
soldiers. In some cities,
there were demonstrations. Raised voices.
Sticks & stones. Stun guns.

There was kicking, hair-pulling,
names were called.
It was anarchy —
                    we got
a taste for it, & we returned
the next day & the next,

to play until the inevitable
call to supper, to stumble, fall,
break open our scabs,
exhaust our toychests, & sing

the hymns of our sponsors.

REVEILLE

A dark Wednesday,
    somewhere in the continuum,

it's raining,
      as my deranged uncle explains his theory

that someday we'll all hear voices
whispering, calling, carrying,

all the voices telling us all that has ever
been voiced

        that noise is energy that never dies
that even as he is telling you this he is
adding to the energy field

        that as he plays
his trumpet over the inaudible trumpet
solos of the past in effect he adds himself

like a layer of silt over the previous
deposits

    that there's a chorus
          down
      under there

of the accumulated reveilles & taps
& charges & scales & all the original
performances & practices, say, of Handel's
Messiah, or Satchmo reigning in the Quarter,

& the trumpet flourish that brought down Jericho,

so cacophonously packed into the background
of the air that our ears become insensitive
to all but the freshest additions

                it survives
in a way that only an archeologist
of silence would be able to appreciate
& yet it survives

   & someday a recording
device will be devised to isolate & playback

Shakespeare's Macbeth its opening night

Whitman composing his leaves out loud or even

when Washington at word of the British advance
curses out Lord Cornwallis for a bastard son
of a navy whore…

it would edit out the birth
cries & the death cries, the explosions & the long,
long intervals of suffering

                    it would revise
our understanding of history

                        my uncle
sees no reason he should bother to age & die

he pulls his trumpet out of its case
& makes
his deranged contribution

MIKE ALEXANDER offers warm thanks to his wife, K.A. Thomas. Previous chapbooks include *Ampersand* (1990), *References* (1996), *January Y2K Blues* (1999), *Blinded by Absinthe* (2004) & *We Internet in Different Voices* (2010, Modern Metrics).

The locales traversed in the Re:Enactment sequence follow the progress of Washington's Retreat Route, November 20, 1776.

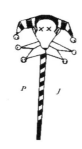

The following poems have previously appeared:

"Du Temps Perdu" in *Abridged 0-22*
"City Life" in *Alabama Literary Review*
"Canticle of the Seventh Month" & "Reveille"
　　　　　　　　　　in *American Poetry Monthly*
"Wax" in *Arkansas Review*
"Templo El Refugio" in *Borderlands*
"Camden Aquarium" & "Paper Dolls" in *Curbside Review*
"Monument Park" in *The Flea*
"Sirens Answer" in **Hand Luggage Only** (Open Poetry Ltd).
"Fermata" in the **Houston Poetry Fest Anthology**
"In Stasis" in *Iron Horse Literary Review*
"What's at Stake" in *the Magazine of Speculative Poetry*
"Ms. Pacman" in *Measure*
"Vegetal Christ" in *Medulla Review*
"Lethe" & "Decoder Ring" in *Mipoesias*
"Prolegomenon," "The Closter Horseman," & "New Bridge"
　　　　　　　　　　in *Newark Review*
"Talk" in *North River Review*
"Crazy Jane & the Crack Pipe" in *Raintown Review*
"Aquarius" in *Sensations Magazine*
"Shahrazad" in *Scheherezade's Bequest*
"Theatre" in *Texas Observer*
"Cornucopia" in *Texas Review*
"Charybdis" in *Znine* & **The Weight of Addition**
　　　　　　　　　　(Mutabilis Press)